THE ILLUMINANT

THE ILLUMINANT

(POEMS)

ABDUL WAHAB LAWAL

National Library of Nigeria Cataloguing-in-Publication Data

Cover design by: *Akila Jibrin*
Cover Photo: *Johannes Plenio (Pexels)*

Printed and Published in Nigeria by:

Words Rhymes & Rhythm Limited
No. 2, Adekunle Tijanni Street, Hillview Estate, Arab Road, Kubwa, Abuja, Nigeria.
08169027757, 08060109295
www.wrr.ng.

DEDICATION

I dedicate this book to:
     God, The One who enabled this;
     Love, the reason we live;
     Life, the pathway in which we dream
     and become; and
     You, for every word you read from it

"Look for
the answer
inside your
question"

– Rumi

GOD

"READ!"
In the name of your Lord.
You shall read of God.
You shall reek of God.
And you shall be of God.

A man bows down to God.
Kissing the earth
He whispers his prayers
To the heavens, in utmost futility
For his eyes do not see
His Blessing, praying and weeping
Behind him effortlessly.

Man thinks of God.
He thinks of God
And he wonders.
He wonders and ponders.
And God is God
He sees and He knows.

And God kisses you
With love and life each day.
But you, like most humans
Do not think.

And God kisses you
With love and life each day
But you, like most humans
Are not wise.

And when we write of God
We scribe of A Being beyond
And when we write of God
We scribe of An Entity Most Loving.
Or how do we describe Him?
He who kisses us with life and love every morning.

I have been to realms beyond
And, each time
The question asked was
"Why are you here?"
And every morning
When my soul breathes
I have my answer.

When man thinks about his future
He tries to look beyond
He tries to navigate
Like he sees beyond.
God watches him
Like a director watching
As his characters perform.

The hero understands the forces behind him.
The villain thinks he has all the powers.
So the director is intrigued
As the clown makes a joke of his acts
And the tragic hero neglects the director.

This act is like every other act
The characters forget and neglect the script.
They think they know better.
At the end, they fail.

A man who knows God must be patient
To be able to see clearly
The things that are obscure
For he trusts the Writer of his destiny.

For the love of sanity
I run from this world
But she runs after me
With might and zeal
Acknowledging and wanting me.
Still, I work tirelessly
Seducing the next
Using one stone to kill two birds
But not without His grace and mercy
All for the love of eternity.

Our path to God
Is a mirror
That shows us who we are
And it is in finding
And knowing God
That we begin to live truly
As a life devoid of its essence
Dies before the arrival of death.

When Shams speaks of God
He nudges Rumi
When Rumi speaks of God
He opens his soul.

When God loves someone
He makes them wonderfully different.
When God loves someone
He tests them.
When God loves someone
He guides them.
When God loves someone
He shows them the way.
When God loves someone
He makes them depend on Him.
When God loves someone
He makes them wonderfully different.

I have seen God
In the eyes of man
And within their hearts
I have felt God.
But when I hear tales of God
From the waggling tongues of man
I become dumb and deaf:
I cannot talk
I cannot hear
But God is God
And Man is but man.

Man is what he sees and hears.
He is the whisperings he acknowledges
The fears that engulf him
And the hope he feeds himself.

The sounds made by birds
Incongruent as they seem
Their meanings unknown to me...
The trees sway
And I look, in dire need of saturation

I seek perfection in this imperfection
For I seek God in everything.

In finding our purpose
We ask questions
From ourselves.
We do not listen
To what our soul says
For we do not know
And cannot hear
Our soul calling us to God.

Nothing brings peace
More than the realisation
That nothing worldly
Can give eternal bliss.

What a bittersweet realisation
That nothing material
Can give eternal happiness.

Let us not forget why we drown;
It is because of faith we drown.
Let us not frown.
It is from drowning
We learn the value of swimming.

The night holds a key
Close to her navel.
Her navel is close to
The heavens.
The heavens ask
But you bask
At night.

We tag the heavens along
So we don't get lost...

Of man's path,
He is what he sees
And he becomes where he journeys.

And when you tour the world alone
You'd one day be at a standstill.

After years of roaming and touring
You **will** eventually realise
That there is a greater beauty
Than the beauty of this world:
      It is the beauty embedded in the hearts of
      humans.

The blue carpeted sky
That I see today
Makes me wonder.
The flying birds
That I see today
Make me ponder.

I do not often
Wonder and ponder.

True love
Blinds its eyes
And deafens its ears
Just for its aim
To stand the test of time.

Love seduces and teaches
Every heart
That ogles her.

She says
    "To love is to be dependent
    And to not love,
    Is to be insane".

In between things we seek
Lies what we do not see.
For we are blind, blinded...

In between why we crave
Lies what we do not hear
For we are deaf, deafened...

By what makes us breathe.

If we love now
Passionately, passionately
Will the love not one day exude?
Will we not be left
With shattered hopes
And broken promises
Of what was never meant to be?

Àgbéké
Will you eventually leave him for me?
Like he left Àshàbí for you?

When he falls out of love
And begins to love another
Will you eventually leave him for me?

When his love finally expires
Will you come to me?
So we can build a home with loyalty and
appreciation?

Leave him for me
For this love they say is never enough.

The fear
always
is the hand
you hold.

Take me home
Into its breast
Where you nest:
A place I shall call home.

Take me home
Into its chest
Where you rest:
A place I shall call home.

Take me home
Into its eyes
Where you see:
A place I shall call home.

Take me home
In its heart
Where you love:
A place I shall call home.

Take me home
To your father
Who mothers your heart:
A place I shall call home.

What love
does is to
light the way

To show you
And brighten
the way

Where there seems
to be
No way.

After a while
We sing along
Where we belong.
After a while
We sing along
Where we do not belong.

Humans wait ashore
Awaiting the ocean;
Their life long partner.
These humans wear the fate
Of a bedridden patient
Craving the lovely hands of death;
Of peace and relief.
But there is another life in the grave
And every ocean brings a storm ashore.

And what holds our tongues
when our hearts beat for another?
Such incandescence that regurgitates itself
from one heart to another – such miracle and
ecstasy; pure magic!

And
And you,
My, my love
You, you make my words skip.

I felt you in my heart today
Like I did yesterday.
In between yesterday & today
Lies a revelation –
> This is how it starts and ends
> Until the day you leave
> And all your memories will leave behind
> Is a welt on my heart.

Love
Beyond the emotion
Is the choice we make:
    To stay
    And to always stay.

Love
Beyond the pain
Beyond the comfort
Beyond the affection
Is the choice we make:
    To stay
    And to always stay.

There is a perfect picture
Of home
In my head.

You are home.
You are my home.

And when you affixed your hands
In mine
I knew you were my shore
And I, your ocean.

And remember
Love alone won't keep you
In love
Till the end of time.

To all, she was his heroine
And for him, she was divine
His true complement.
She was God sent
God's ultimate gift.
She was his answered prayers
Hovering around him, saying
"I was carved from your ribs
Made of you
You, of God."

I have written poems
Of you
For you
And to you
But just like time
You glide
And just like everyman
I am waiting for Godot.

For Akanke

Have you ever been told?
You're pure magic to behold.

When you're away
I am faraway
From myself.

You exude with bliss
Pure ecstasy in my soul
As if that's not enough
My heart calls your names
During the busiest part of the day
Like today,
When I held my soul
Levitating the universe.

I heard my heart
Calling out to you
As if you were his very own;
When two souls align
They sing along a song
A song only them can hear
And look in awe
Finding meaning to what gives them joy.

When you're away,
I am faraway
From myself.

Your face symbolises *jannah*
Take us home.
Will you?

Love is
Devotion
Commitment
Venerated with
Zeal and sincerity.

We are on a journey:
Holding hands is what we do
Until we get tired
And leave to hold another hand.

We are on a journey:
Eating affection from heart to heart
Is what we do
Until we die of hunger.
We eat affection.

We are on a journey:
Pain is what we know
For that is why we are on a journey
Until we reach the promise land.

My eyes see that
They cannot see
So they bribed my soul.

My soul sees that
She can see
So she became my eyes and ears.

My heart dazes herself every time
And each time she does
She is an intoxicant for a purpose:
To know and to learn
That the heart does not
Own or control herself.

And by love
We mean peace of mind.

Of all the love that exists
None is greater than the love for the unseen.
For what a person sees and then likes
        Isn't often what the soul needs
            And what the soul needs
                Isn't often seen through the eyes.

I write for you
Words I could never write for myself.
It is totally true that love transcends man
Forget the simple words
I'd *grandise* my love for you
After which I'd *educritain* people about love.

I write for you
Bit by bit
I write for you
Love with love.

MADE UP WORDS.
- Grandise - to make grand
- Educritian - to educate, critique and entertain.

How can you seek happiness
From another being that seeks happiness?

To express love is never to impress.
It is to purely define
How a river flows back and forth
With such clarity of purpose.

That clarity of purpose gives hope
That love is with purpose:
A purpose that stands and bears
A purpose that resists and persists
A purpose that lasts till all else fades.

The true nature of a man
Is that which he acts
And tells himself:
I am this and that.

The true nature of a man
Is the war he fights
And no one knows:
I hate this and that.

The true nature of a man
Is the love he craves
That which his heart has chosen:
I like this and that.

The true nature of a man
Is the way he sees
And makes his choices:
I want this and that.

The true nature of a man
Is the person he loves
And reflects upon his soul:
I am this not that.

Àwèlé

My love for you
Is like my love for similes
It stems from like
And gravitates into love.

Àwèlé
As the moon endears
The night with its light
My love will illuminate
Your heart with its might.
And at night, when your heart is aglow
Because of my love for you
We'd see through eternity
A realm inexistent to feeble minds.

Àwèlé
I will love you
As though loving you alone means to live
And to live without loving you equals death.

Man's greatest assets
Are his soul
And the other soul
He accepts to journey with his soul.

Àbíké
You thought it was only in the days of your
forefathers
That love never dies

Àbíké
You asked why love dies easily now

It's simple
Today's love is a showcase
Between lovers to the world.

*It was
During one of those late
Nights
When our misty eyes
Drizzled resilience
That we found out
Nothing defines love
More than devotion.*

*When a man tours the world
And he achieves greatness
Without being loved
He becomes an entity
Without a soul.*

*True greatness isn't what is acquired.
True greatness is bestowed.
To be truly loved is a divine blessing
Its feeling is inimitable.*

Oh Beautiful One,
The things you make me feel
Gift endless bliss.

Only eternity should feel this way.

He who loves truly
Fights a war:
A sincerely passionate war
Against time.

Little by little
They forget
Why they live
Like most married men
Forget how to love.

The ache-easer, the bliss
The soul of my forest – Amal.

Life

How often do we peck our hearts
And tell our souls *"cheers!"*?
Life is a parable:
Our dreams are prophecies.

How often do we sing lullabies
And scribe with ours hands, dirges?
Life is a play:
Our beings are actors.

How often do we get intoxicated by nothingness
And play seductively with this façade?
Life is a chameleon:
Her nature is bewildering.

The mouth of an old man
Takes you through his glory and regret .
Beyond his experience
His tongue reeks of his life.

I do not know what gives a man away
Than his mouth…
Well, maybe his eyes
And the way he looks
Or his body, and the way he walks.

I have seen children smile like old men.
I have seen old men smile like children.
Life is what happened to a child.
A child eager to be a man
Becomes a man wishing
To turn back the hands of time.

A child is the father of a man.
A good father or not
He becomes not what life teaches him
But what he learns from life.

DOPAMINE
That we eat affection
And live in depression.

We live our lives
In cubicles
And the gods
Of this planet
Reward us
With affection and depression.

LIVING
Happiness is the cap you wear.
Sadness is the secret you hide.

PURSUITS
And you see that you can see.
And you see that you see not.

When we write of love
We write of something that lives.
So we write bashfully
Of something with eternal life.

When we write of man
We write of something that dies.
So we write regretfully
Of something with a fixed span.

And when we write of death
We write of something that dies.
So we write indifferently
Of something with(out) hope.

My friend is a sage
And I am not.
He tells me stories of destruction
And I sing to him pleasures in destruction.
He talks of God
And I talk of the Devil.
He writes of love
And I scribe of envy.

My friend is a dreamer, a believer.
I am a thinker, a conceiver.

My friend adores saints
But I don't believe they exist.
My friend hates evildoers
And I think they matter.

This world is not for saints
Or evildoers:
Sanity is for those in between.

Life is a journey home
But where is home?

Knowledge is light
But where is the knowledge?

Wisdom is power
But where is the wisdom?

Life is a question mark
Archived into commas
You cannot totally grasp.
And that is her power.

Yours is to dance
In sync with her hugs and blows.

Life is like a woman
That loves you, and yet frustrates you
And you are a man
You cannot not love a woman –
That is life.

*"So, adopt the pace of nature
Her secret is patience."*

Cries. Smiles.
Same event.

Life teaches a lesson
A tough lesson
That, at times, your fate
Is not in your hands.

CATHARSIS
Soft cries, teary eyes
Eyes eyeing the earth
For dearth of death...

Feigned smiles. Penury's aisle
Concealed *rima oris*
For who cares.

Wet your eyes with willing waters
Make your demand your supply
And placate your heart with words within.

How do we
Teach our sons
To be better
Than their fathers
When all we do is work?

How do we
Teach our daughters
To be better
Than their mothers
When all we do is work?

At some point
We forget where we are.
The world smiles us
And we smile back.

An old man once said:
>	*"When a child gets a glimpse of heaven*
>	*He forgets there are better heavens.*
>	*And just like his forefathers*
>	*He shall forget to die*
>	*Before his death."*

Inequality:
Life's greatest bread
Served with equity – perfection!

PERSEVERANCE
    Life is a stage
        That stages herself
           Seducing her own
               And building her own.

For the words we eat
And the vacuums we fill
For the love we kill
And the wrath we dish
For the beauty we hide
And the fear we wear
For the life we fear
And the hearts we gore
For the pain we drip
And the love we leave
For the things we become
And the things we've forgone

For life is a dynamic compass
One that shows you Paradise
Just so you pass through hell.

And your big soul, for a little path
A little, little path, an obscure path.
And this is not your soul.
This is not your path.

Wayfarer!
The journey – this journey
Is of dynamic, brilliant fallibilities.

Fall and rise
Again and again
Just ensure your rise after every fall.

And remember
No man is infallible.

A stranger is an unknown planet
That shows another stranger its planet
Real or surreal.

The atlas to this stranger's planet
Is the cap
On his heart.
His heart is the universe
And the cap is The Truth.

The future is embedded
With pain and pleasure.
This certainty is his sanity.
The present is ironically the future.

Dibú smiles as if Death is his friend
And tells everyman with a head and a heart
That the future is the present:
The best of you are those
Who understand the recipe of pain
And live life without complaining
About its features – *its ups and downs.*

Tell me of memories
Dead and buried
Murdered and covered
Like corpses beneath the earth.

What is life without pain
...paradise before eternity.
So, love the somber nights
They are divine constructs.
Everything that exists
Will one day be no more.

PATIENCE
A step at a time
        A goal at a time
                A time at a time.

                Patience is a father
            A father who is no time's fool
        A father who mothers time
A father who breastfeeds time.

FOR THE CAUSE OR APPLAUSE

Of the glory that wept
The sun burnt the eyes
Leaving it for dead
For the ears tiptoed towards
Man's *rima oris*
To take a sip of pleasure

It rained turbulent blessings
The words caressed the heart
And the heart kissed the words
Enchantingly, the words drowned the heart.

And man
Being a man
Died of thirst
In an ocean.

Take a bike to heaven
Swim beneath the heart:
Whatever you see
Whatever you hear
Dream well
This is all a dream.

In between a man's soul
Are the blessings

He plunges away
He makes a way
While wasting away.
He plays home
He plays away

Like a seer
Unsure of his own future
He forecasts a game
While staking his future.
He wins
Yet he loses

He wins the Devil's dough
And loses Heaven's bow
He forecasts the future
Yet murders his future.

You need not be told
You need not be wise to know
That what he makes of today
Is what tomorrow holds.

He pictured a quiet life
He envisaged a busy life

Quiet or busy
Happily, justly
Live a quiet life happily
And a busy life, justly.

Thunder struck
I woke
The sun rose
I slept

How can you fear Hell
And still toss away Paradise?

CONTENTMENT

After our prayers are answered
They lose value with time
The job we craved
The spouse we yearned for
Everything falls on *by the way* side.

We seek more
And all we have becomes nothing
As though we never toiled to have them.
Man is so forgetful a being!

Everything we have is a blessing and a test:
A blessing bestowed upon us by God
And a test, to know how grateful we'd be
For being blessed.

And remember
Lust is momentary

Its way offers no fruitful fecundity
There, souls collide
And drown in a filthy well.

To dwell in Heaven
And play with inimitable Hell
Is relishing Paradise before Eternity.

On your way up the stairs
You'd meet ambiguous stares
And unwanted smears:
Whether or not danger looms
Whether or not success booms.

In the eyes of man
You'd see uncertainty
Like a wench unsure of her child's paternity.

Every day and time
You know there is no time
But as each day passes by
You wonder when you'd say goodbye
To the ambiguous stares
And unwanted smears

Do you ever say goodbye?

And lust
Consumed them,
Disguised as
An inimitable pleasure.

CERTITUDE

To those who fatten themselves
On envy and hatred
And measure their happiness
With the sorrow and fall of others
I say:

> Time and men glide
> Like ageing skin
> And how it wears men.

> So shall you see straws at the end of your
> tunnel
> Should you not cringe in fear
> And glide towards contentment.

Family is gold:
Even when the hearts get cold
And power lines are down
Family is gold.

With days of stupendous blues
And drizzling oceanic hues
From faraway land
Family is gold.

And when you see no one
To hold your hands
To touch your cheeks
And make you giggle
Family is gold.

Family isn't just gold
Family is life.
It is when old age arrives
And we rethink, seeing straws
And sanity settles.

But it would be too late
For family to be gold
For family was never the way of our life.

It is from the mouths of man
You hear the unfair tales of God
The mouths of man
Ever ready, ever prepared
To speak of that which
Their fickle minds
Can never grasp.

It is these mouths you fear.
It is these ungraceful mouths that scare you.
When these mouths run garbage about God
Would their ungraceful mouths
Not gracefully ridicule your being?

It is what we feel
That breaks us.

To define a way to feel
Is to understand
What and how to feel.

It is what we know
That makes us
Know there are things
Best left unknown:
It is how we stay sane.

We talk
And talk
That we forget
The talk.

Day by day
The home unwears its fragrance
And loses its feeling of stupendous harmony
Till there exists a vacuum
Caused by tired inhabitants
Who now seek another haven beyond their home.

Until we know why once loving inhabitants
Get tired and forgetful
We pray for sanity and serenity
For insane inhabitants and their homes.

The things that make you happy
Are usually the things
That make you very sad.

So, be careful about the things you love.

The reality is:
    Life is not the reality.

She, the rib
That complements a man –
That wonderful entity
It is that rib
You bend and spoil
An entity carved by God!

How dare you!
You, a thing of the dust
Think so lowly
Of such a powerful entity?

Àbèfé
Did you not know?
To love man is to live
The rest of your life with uncertainty.

The dream is free
Why and how do you dream cheap dreams?

Do you not know love at first sight?
It is lust charging through its pores.

Never you yearn for praises
For it isn't worth the yearning.

Never you crave the *likes*
For it can later turn into spite.

Never you stop loving and soaring
For it illuminates the soul.

Never you forget why you began
For that keeps you going when down.

…most importantly never you stop penning
For service to humanity is the greatest of all.

These things you seek
When you get them
Will you be able to keep them?

Man is ungrateful.
He lies to himself
That the things he wants
Are the only things he wants.
He lies that he never wants more.

So, when he has it all
He scratches his head
And points to another man's property
Like a womanizer searching for prey
He forgets he's unworthy of a wife:
He looks for death
Just after he's been blessed.

These things you seek
When you get them
Will you be able to keep them?

We live in our heads
And sleep in our minds
After several lampoons
Of drowsy imaginations.

We dream in our hands
And sleep with our feet
After several dunks
Fascinating our thoughts.

The dreams
Success, an ocean
In our heads.

We dream on
To act our greatest challenge.

Our lives aren't meant for sightseeing.

"The apple in my pouch is better than yours
And the orange in your yard is better than mine"

How would you define better?
What is better?
What is good for you?
Is it good for me?

Man knows not what he needs
But the things he gets
Are the things he needs:
They are good for him and him alone
However he tags them – 'good' or 'bad.

What does he know?
What does man know of God?
That he desires what another man has
What does man know of destiny?
That he craves another man's destiny.

The things you get are the things you need,
Be contented.

THE PROCESS

You, like the sun
Want to shine.
But you, unlike the sun,
Do not revere darkness.

PRIDE

Shall we wash our prideful words off our mouths
As we rid the metaphysical of new bodies and
souls?

No man lives and dies unstained
For he takes blemishes to his grave.
But when he lived here, with us
Did he not for once look at himself with utter
reverence
As would the deuce call himself the way?

The pathway to greatness
Lies in your home.
Everything you seek is seeking you:
For what you are, you reflect
And what you exude comes back.

A man is a sacrificial lamb
And only a responsible man lives honorably.

Do you ask that same question?
The one everyone asks
"Why am I here?"

Do you get a fitting answer?
The one everyone needs
Why are you here?

You are here to think
To think and wonder.
You are here to act
To act and justify.

Why are you here?
"You, listen, the answer is inside your question".

Your soul & heart
Embody your whole.

Whatever & however you are
You are the light & love you seek.

"Then will you not see?"

– Qur'ān 51:21 (*b*)